WHAT MEN DO BECAUSE OF POWER: the obsession of men and its event ward result.

By: Clayton L. Anderson

TABLE OF CONTENTS

CHAPTER 1: THE THOUGHTS OF POWER

Power is often defined as the capacity to initiate, stop, or influence events; the choice of whether to act or not.

A person's legal right to decide and change (at his or her own will) the rights, obligations, liabilities, and other legal relationships that apply to him or her.

the capacity to do an action or behave in a certain manner, notably as a trait or talent.

the capability or power to control or influence how others behave or how events unfold. Power is defined as the ability of A to shape B's conduct such that B complies with A's desires.

Many academics have offered several definitions of power. Here are a few prevalent explanations:

Kingsley Davis asserts that "power is the determination of others' conduct in pursuit of one's own objective."

"Power represents the relative Weights of conduct by a member in a social structure," says Sheriff.

Weber defined power as the likelihood that one actor (person or group) within a social connection is in a position to carry out his or her own will in the face of opposition, independent of the foundation for this likelihood.

"Power is only the degree of the capacity to manage others so that they would accomplish what they wished to do," says Green.
Power is a complicated strategic condition in a certain society's social framework, according to Michel Foucault.

"The capacity to obtain these distinctive skills is what allows leaders to influence subordinates and peers through managing organizational resources," claim Patrick J. Montana and Bruce H. Charnov.

Even if it exists, power may not be utilised. Hence, it is capability or potential. Power may exist, but it cannot be imposed. Power's relationship to reliance is perhaps its most significant feature.

The more dependent B is on A, the more dominant A is in the relationship. The options B sees and the value B puts on the alternative(s) that A controls are the foundations of dependence. Only if someone has control over what you want can they claim to have influence over you.

10 Power Sources
The possession of authority and influence over others is referred to as having power. Depending on how it is utilized, power is a tool that may have

beneficial or harmful effects on a group, nation, community, or even a family.

What source does the electricity have?
What exactly gives a person or a group power over others?
In order to respond to these inquiries, we first divide the bases or sources of power into two broad categories formal and personal before further subdividing each into more granular groups.

The paper "The Bases of Power," written by American sociologists John French and Bertram Raven, is recognized as the standard for categorizing power in organizations. They located a few power sources.

10 sources of power include

Formal Authority
Legitimate Power.
Expert Power.

Referent power.
Use of Force/Coercive power
Power Reward.
Knowledge/information Power
Adapter power.
Political Influence
Charismstic power

Let's go through 10 different power sources.

Formal Power: A person's formal power is determined by their standing within an organization. Formal power may result from the capacity to compel compliance, recognize formal authority, or maintain information control.

The official authority is dependent on rank, such as that of the captain or fire chief.

Legitimate Power: In formal groupings and organizations, access to one or more power bases is perhaps most often gained via one's structural position. We refer to this as legitimate authority.

Positional power is another name for legitimate authority. It is based on a person's standing inside the organizational structure. The individual in a position of power must be seen as having earned it honestly in order for it to be used successfully. The CEO of a firm is an illustration of legitimate authority.

Expert Power: Influence exercised as a result of exceptional knowledge, skill, or competence. Having knowledge or competence in a certain field gives one expert power.

These individuals are highly valued by organizations for their ability to solve problems.

Ownership of expert power often serves as a springboard for other types of power, such legal authority.

Referent Power: Referent power is the ability to influence others by identification with someone who has attractive qualities or assets.

You may have authority over me if I admire, respect, and like you because I want to please you. It comes from the interpersonal connections that an individual forges with others inside the company.

When people respect and appreciate someone, that person has reference power. Referent power is also generated through a person's close relationships with influential figures in a community or organization's hierarchy.

Coercive Power: The capacity to exert pressure on others by threats, penalties, or sanctions is known as coercive power.
Hence, coercive power is the capacity of a person to penalize, dismiss, or chastise their subordinates.

By making sure that people follow the rules and expectations, coercive authority aids in controlling the conduct of your subjects.

Reward Power: Reward power is the polar opposite of coercive power. Individuals obey orders or requests from others because doing so results in advantageous outcomes; consequently, one who is able to give out incentives that others deem desirable will have control over those people.

These incentives may be monetary, such as determining pay rates, increases, and bonuses, or they may be non-financial, such as acknowledgment for achievement, promotions, engaging job assignments, sociable coworkers, and preferred work hours or sales territory.

Those who hold positions of authority tend to have an impact on others' behavior, whether in a group or in society as a whole. When applied effectively, reward power powerfully drives subjects and followers.

Yet when used unfairly, reward power may severely undermine followers' morale and reduce their productivity.

Informational Power: Informational power is the ability to get information that is required or desired. It results from restrictions over and access to information. This is a transitory power with little potential for credibility or impact.

Yet, it is difficult to maintain this power for very long, and ultimately, this knowledge will be made public.
This approach shouldn't be used in the long run.

Connection power is the ability to obtain influence via friendship or simple familiarity with a strong someone.

The key to this strength is networking. I will have power if I can establish a relationship with the person I wish to approach.

Individuals who use this power form significant alliances with others. It comes naturally to him or her to build these kinds of relationships with others and bring them together into coalitions that offer him or her significant connection power.

Political Influence: This influence comes from a group's backing. It results from a leader's capacity to influence individuals and social structures in order to win their loyalty and support.

It grows in all state-owned organizations, particularly when a certain political party is in control and its adherents exhibit influence in various facets of the institutions.

Leaders may influence people and get access to certain resources from the organization by leveraging their political power.

Charismatic Power: Charismatic power is an extension of referent power derived from a person's character and communication preferences.

Because they can articulate a compelling vision, take personal risks, exhibit environmental and follower sensitivity, and are willing to engage in behavior that most people would view as unconventional, charismatic leaders can inspire others to follow them.

However, many organizations will have charismatic individuals who, despite not holding official leadership positions, can influence others due to their valor.

The aforementioned bases/types of power are frequently used in a wide variety of organizations, nations, societies, communities, etc.

However, it is true that not every power can be found in a single organization. Powers are used in a variety of ways depending on the organization, the occasion, the person, the circumstance, etc.

The following factors determine the three possible outcomes of a person's attempted use of power:

the source of the ruler's power
the operationalization of that power base; and
particular traits of the follower
When a follower empathizes with a leader and consents to the leader's power play, commitment is more likely to occur. When the subordinate is prepared to accept the leader's wishes, compliance is likely the result, provided that acceptance does not need more work on the side of the subordinate.

When a subordinate is hesitant to follow orders and may even intentionally ignore them to prevent the leader's goals from being fulfilled, resistance is the typical result.

sources of a leader's sway types of results
Commitment Compliance Resistance

Referent Strength Probably if the leader believes the request to be significant. Maybe, if the leader believes the request to be inconsequential. If the request is for something that may hurt the leader, it is possible.

expert strength Likely if the request is strong and the followers agree with the objectives of the assignment. Maybe if the request is strong but the subordinates are uninterested in the objectives of the assignment. It's possible if the boss acts haughtily and insultingly or if the team members disagree with the work objectives.

Authentic Power is Possible if the request is respectful and very pertinent. If a request or order is deemed to be valid, it is likely Maybe if haughty demands are made or the request seems inappropriate.

Power Reward Possible if done subtly and with great care. Likely if applied in a robotic, emotionless manner. Possible if applied in a manipulative, haughty manner.

Powerful Coercion very improbable Possible, if used in a constructive, non-punitive manner Probably if used in an aggressive or deceitful manner.

the use of referent power

Referent power, as shown in the illustration, has several advantages for a leader. Using the following actions, leaders may create and keep referent power:

Fairly and equally to the subordinate

Identifying the interests of the subordinate

Show consideration for the needs and emotions of the subordinates.

Choose followers who are similar to the leader.

Be a proactive, inspiring role model.

Using Expertise

In order to win over the subordinates, the leader may also benefit greatly from expert authority. A leader should: in order to achieve and maintain a high degree of expert power.

bolster his or her reputation as an expert
preserve professional credibility
Be assertive and decisive in your actions.
Stay current and informed.
Acknowledge your subordinates' worries.
Don't put your subordinates' self-esteem at danger.
Utilizing legal authority
By officially and repeatedly asking subordinates to do actions that advance the goals of the group, leaders exert legitimate authority.

The following are some guidelines for the exercise of lawful power:

Be kind and respectful to subordinates at all times.

Keep a posture of confidence in the rightful position of authority.

Provide detailed directions, then confirm knowledge by checking in later.

Make sure your request is suitable.

Provide the request's justifications.

Observe the correct organizational channels.

Use your legal authority often and persistently.

Show consideration for the worries of subordinates.

Reward Power in Use
For both the leader and the subordinate, reward power is often the simplest and most gratifying power basis. By following a few fundamental rules, such as the ones listed below, the reward power base's potential values may be maximized:

Check output and adherence.
Make realistic and fair demands to subordinates.

Make only morally and appropriately sound demands.

Provide and give out prizes that your subordinates want.

Give only prizes that are trustworthy.

Using Coercive Power: The most challenging and painful kind of power to use. There will almost probably be some animosity as a consequence of the use of compulsion, and in certain instances there may even be widespread anger and revenge.

The referent power of the leader tends to diminish even with little discontent. The most a leader can expect from coercion is obedience, and that is only achievable if compulsion is used in a constructive, non-punitive way.

But, the leader must understand that resistance is the most frequent result whenever coercive authority is used. The following actions must be taken by the leader to reduce opposition and foster compliance:

Ensure that all subordinates are aware of all regulations.
Before punishing subordinates, issue a warning.
Punishment should be applied consistently and uniformly.
Before taking any action, make sure you completely comprehend the circumstance.
continue to be a credible leader.
Make sure the penalty is appropriate for the offense.
Always discipline privately.
Leaders should take great care to limit the numerous unfavorable effects of their actions while using coercive authority, particularly when they are inexperienced.

The commander runs the risk of winning the battle but losing the war by reprimanding a particular subordinate. Punishment must be applied with a unique balance of encouragement, sincerity, and severity.

Power Principles in Personal Relationships
We are aware that there are several forms of power as well as ideals.

As a perception, power
The Least Interest and Dependency Principle Power.
Relational concept of power.
Resource-Based Power.
Enabling or Disabling Power
The prerogative of power.
The guidelines are covered below;

As a Perception, Power
In the sense that some people can have objective power while still having difficulty influencing others, power is a perception. People are more

likely to perceive someone as powerful when they exhibit power cues and act decisively and forcefully.

Some people gain influence despite not overtly displaying domineering traits.

The Least Interest and Dependent Power Principle
More influence in the partnership belongs to the one that has less to lose.

Dependency power states that those who are dependant on their spouse or relationship are weaker, particularly if they are aware that their partner is not committed and may leave them.

The sort of connections and possibilities someone may have if they weren't in their present relationship are referred to as the quality of alternatives in the interdependence theory.

The level of relational power and interest in the connection are inversely correlated.

Relational concept of power
Power is a social construct. How much power a person has in relation to their spouse is often at question in this situation. In intimate, fulfilling partnerships, partners often have varied, ongoing influences on one another.

Often, a conflict for resources is what power as a resource-based power looks like. Power battles become more fierce and lengthy as resources become more valuable and scarce.

According to the scarcity theory, when resources are few or in great demand, individuals are at their most powerful. Nevertheless, power only results from a limited resource if that resource is valued inside a partnership.

Enabling or Deactivating Power

Power may be turned on or off. According to research, dominating conduct that demonstrates social skills as opposed to intimidation increases the likelihood that an individual will have a long-lasting impact on others.

Having personal strength shields you from external pressure, undue influence from others, and/or stressful circumstances.

Individuals who express themselves via self-assurance and expressive, composed conduct often succeed in their aims and sustain healthy relationships.

When it results in negative communication patterns, power may be incapacitating.

As a Prerogative, Power
According to the prerogative principle, the partner with greater power has the authority to set and enforce regulations. Powerful individuals are less likely to suffer consequences when they breach

social standards, break interpersonal boundaries, or manipulate relationships. These activities could increase the strong person's reliance on their position.

In addition, the dominant party has the right to control both verbal and nonverbal communications. They are more adept at starting talks, changing the subject, interjecting, initiating physical contact, and wrapping up discussions than less strong individuals.

Power Approaches Based on Circumstances: For instance, Pfeffer just asserts that having power depends on being in the "correct" position. The leader is at the proper place or position when they have the following qualities:

control over assets like finances, physical spaces, and positions that may be utilized to build more fans and friends.
formally sanctioned.

Such astute observations are supported by certain studies, while some study results also lead to other conclusions, such as the following:

The more professionally oriented a group's members are, the more relative influence referent power has on them.
Lower-ranking participants are more likely to acquire power related to this task the less work and interest high-ranking players are ready to devote to a task.

Ultimately, internalization will occur since it is consistent with the person's value system.

Yet, as the image demonstrates, the agent must be credible and relevant in order for individuals to absorb them.

The best method of exercising power is this one.

For instance, Kelman discovered that internalized power had a long-lasting effect on the participants in his investigations. The development of metrics for compliance, identification, and internalization has proven challenging for researchers.

This power structure does, however, have a lot of application to how and when managers and supervisors influence their subordinates. Many must rely on compliance for internalization to take place because they lack referent power or are not appealing.

According to Kelman's study, internalization produced the greatest long-term effects and did not need salience or monitoring, as shown by the model.

To put it another way, what is often thought of as leadership has more to do with influencing others to do more than merely obey, such as to connect with the leader and, even better, internalize the goals of the influence effort.

In today's highly independent, flat societies with cultures of openness, empowerment, and trust, this internalization would be particularly desirable.

Influenceability of Power's Targets
The majority of discussions of power assume that influence is exerted unilaterally from the actor to the target.

The broader social-cognitive viewpoint used in this work, however, makes it more evident that power includes a reciprocal interaction between the actor and the target.

Examining a few of the target's traits can help you better understand the power connection. The following traits have been shown to be particularly crucial to a target's capacity to be persuaded.

Dependency.
Uncertainty.
Personality.
Intelligence.

Gender.\sAge.\sCulture.

Dependency

The resources under the agent's control determine how dependent the target is. Power influence will be strong if reliance is high, or vice versa.

More targets are impacted the more dependent they are on their connection with agents.

Uncertainty

The agent's capacity to be persuaded depends on how convinced or doubtful he is that his action is suitable.

Studies have demonstrated that individuals are more easily persuaded to alter their conduct when they are unsure about whether their actions are suitable or right.

Personality

There is evidence from several research investigations that personality and influenceability are related. For instance, persons who have a hard time with ambiguity or who are really worried are more prone to being swayed.

Intelligence

It has been noted that more intellectual individuals are less vulnerable to the influence brought about by positional authority, even though there is no concrete evidence linking intelligence and influenceability directly.

Gender

There is little evidence to suggest that this is changing, despite the conventional wisdom that women were more prone than males to submit to efforts at persuasion because of the way they were reared.

There is less of a difference in influenceability by gender as women's and society's perspectives on women's roles shift.

Age

According to social psychologists, influence sensitivity rises in early children up to the age of eight or nine, declines with age until adolescence, and then levels off.

Culture A society's cultural norms have a significant effect on how influencing its members are. Targets' capacity to be influenced is influenced by the cultural traits to which they belong.

Those from cultures that value authority, for instance, are more receptive to persuasion than persons from cultures that place less value on authority.

Strength Dynamics
Power is defined as the capacity to affect other individuals and external circumstances. It refers to A's ability to sway B's actions so that B carries out A's instructions.

This concept indicates a dependent connection and a potential that need not be realized in order to be successful. Even if it exists, power may not be utilised. Hence, it is capability or potential.

Power may exist, but it cannot be imposed. Power's relationship to reliance is perhaps its most significant feature. The more dependent B is on A, the more dominant A is in the relationship.

The options B sees and the value B puts on the alternative(s) that A controls are the foundations of dependence. Only if someone has control over what you want can they claim to have influence over you.

Normally, we believe that those with the most influence are also the most persuasive.

As a result, they would often be in favor in a vote.

Nonetheless, there are situations when the result of a choice is clear before it is taken, and people will join the winning team in an effort to avoid being on the losing side.

CHAPTER 2: LEADERSHIP AND THE POWER MATRIX

Leadership and the Power Matrix:

Power acquisition has often been seen as unethical or base. According to Francis Bacon, "The desire for knowledge in excess caused man to fall; the desire for power in excess caused the angels to fall." Then he said, "Knowledge itself is strength." So, according to Bacon, man's pursuit of knowledge is a pursuit of power, which led to his fall.

"You must have pleasure or you shall have strength, said God, you shall not have both," Ralph Waldo Emerson wrote in his diary. Men "quite naturally crave money or power," he said, "and power because it is as good as money." "He who has his thumb on the purse has the authority," Otto Von Bismarck said.

These claims aim to demonstrate the parity of power, wealth, and knowledge. Some individuals think that everyone is evil. Power tends to corrupt, and absolute power corrupts completely, as Lord Acton famously said.

Does any thinking person actually accept this adage, despite the fact that it is often repeated and has an unmistakably learnt ring? To be free, one has to have power. "Liberty is not only a notion, an abstract ideal," observed John Dewey. It is power—specific power that is effective. "Freedom is participation in power," declared Cicero.

The term "empowerment" has recently become a political catchphrase, meaning giving the marginalized authority. Acton's beliefs and those of the other people who distrust authority would be accurate if empowerment were corruptible. If corrupting the innocent was the politicians' secret objective, it would be very Machiavellian.

Power is the capacity to accomplish goals at the time and in the manner desired by the entity holding it, while causing the least amount of trouble. It is neither morally reprehensible nor energizing spiritually. It is impartial.

But, the technique utilized to get electricity and the objectives for which it is employed unquestionably have an impact on the outcome's quality. According to Mao Tse-tung, political authority cannot exist without the use of force and weaponry. Political authority "grows out of the barrel of a rifle," he said. John Quincy Adams, however, asserted that the foundation for political authority is essentially different from that of military might. The country that has the most freedom must obviously be the nation with the most power in relation to its population, he said. "Individual liberty is individual power," he argued. "And because the strength of a society is a mass composed of individual powers." According to

Malcolm X, "Power for freedom is stronger than power for tyranny and oppression."

Power is a prerequisite for freedom. Without freedom, independence is impossible. Yet without independence, living a successful and satisfying life is almost impossible. We must thus look for power.

What are this illusive good's fundamental characteristics? What steps must we take to get it? And how should it be handled after it has been acquired?

"Power may be taken, but it cannot be given," said G. Steinem. Even the act of taking itself is empowering. Hence, acquiring authority cannot be done on someone else's behalf. It must be consciously chosen by a person or group to be theirs, and they must take action to fulfill that choice. This is not to suggest that an environment cannot be established that encourages organizations or people to pursue their own authority. This is both possible and desirable. Yet, neither a person nor a group can live another person's life. Power belongs to those who seize it for themselves. Each tub must stand on its own bottom, as the adage goes.

Power requires individuals who desire it to develop ability since it is the capacity to carry out specified tasks. There is no other option since there is no power without competence. Knowledge is thus one of the main paths to power. Learning the tricks of the trade is beneficial for blind people. Beyond that, it's also crucial to master a body of information that will allow you to compete with others. Yet, having knowledge (or money, for that matter) is insufficient. To guarantee that the blind have authority, there must be something else.

The individual's conviction that it is legitimate for power to live inside them is one component of the power matrix. You may call this conviction "confidence." Another factor is other people acknowledging the blind person's abilities. Without this acknowledgement, whatever power a person has (no matter how enormous) would be dismissed as a myth. Can a blind person become president of the United States or get the Nobel Prize? We haven't yet gotten the credit we deserve if the response is "No," if it's thought that sight is necessary for these tasks. Describe this acceptance as "public understanding." Power may exist with these with aptitude, self-assurance, and public awareness. Yet, obtaining these components requires teamwork; it cannot be done on one's alone. No one in a group can become powerful without the other members of the group also obtaining some strength. Hence, if you want to ensure that a colleague acquires power, work to increase your own. Instead, assist a buddy in order to raise your own. Organized group members help one another, and they rise to prominence far more quickly than individuals without a strong network of allies.

The most influential people have become who they are today by encouraging others to share in their vision for change. They also understand that being kind increases rather than decreases power.

There are other things about the nature of power that may be mentioned. One of them is that power must be used in order for it to be sustained and strengthened, and that using power calls for leadership. The power of a person or an organization is increased to the degree that they execute leadership. This begs the question: What does leadership entail? Energy, inventiveness, excitement, the capacity to sympathize with others, communication skills, and ease in interpersonal connections are just a few of the qualities that are beneficial. Yet, one primary component is more important than the others together. Love is that one quality the willingness to care for lofty ideals and our fellow humans, the willingness to see past others' flaws and idiosyncrasies to the value that each represents, the willingness to wish others well even when they do not wish well for us, and the willingness to understand that being kind to others brings its own rewards. An organization that includes the characteristic of love in its governance increases its power. Naturally, it must be genuine; no pretension will do. And love that is freely offered is at least as strict a taskmaster.

CHAPTER 3: THE POWER OF PSYCHOLOGY IN POLITICS

An academic discipline known as political psychology focuses on the psychological aspect of political life. Its practitioners analyze the intricate and reciprocal link between politics and psychology by using psychological variables like as personality, attitudes, beliefs, values, needs, objectives, and expectations to explain political action. Political psychologists believe that, like all other types of human behavior, political acts are the outcome of interactions between an individual's environment and themselves. Political science, which examines the relationships and interactions between people acting as political agents, is inextricably tied to psychology, which studies human cognition and behavior. The relationship between personality characteristics and political circumstances has piqued the curiosity of political analysts throughout history and throughout cultures. To explain why rulers and subjects think and behave the way they do and how their beliefs and deeds influence politics, they have used a variety of notions and theories. Political psychology therefore emphasizes the crucial role played by psychological elements in determining how well a person responds to diverse contextual and environmental stimuli.

Modern political psychology, which emerged in the years after World Wars I and II, has grown to include a broad range of topics. Its philosophical foundations may be found in the works of renowned American political scientist and communications theorist Harold D. Lasswell (1902–1978). His influential works, including Psychopathology and Politics, World Politics and Personal Insecurity, Politics: Who Gets What, When, and How, Power and Personality, and Power and Society, emphasized the role of social and individual psychological processes perception, motivation, conflict, cognition, learning, socialization, attitude formation, and group dynamics as causal factors affecting politics. The subject of political psychology was initially unidirectional, with a particular emphasis on how the individual psyche impacts political conduct and beliefs, according to Lasswell's groundbreaking work in the area.

Max Horkheimer , Erich Fromm , Herbert Marcuse , and Theodor Adorno , among others, were prominent members of the Institute for Social Research at the University of Frankfurt (the so-called Frankfurt school), who had fled Nazi Germany for the United States. The concept of authoritarian personality, which examines the causal connection between political views and personality types, was developed by these individuals. Adorno and his colleagues at the University of California, Berkeley were inspired by their theories to conduct a groundbreaking empirical study, The Authoritarian Personality (1950), based on the F(ascism)-scale measurement, which connected right-wing authoritarianism with a family pattern of rigidity, discipline, strict rules, and fearful subservience to parental demands. This now-classic study illustrates how certain politically significant components of the mind lead to fascist or authoritarian belief systems while being heavily criticized, especially for its strong reliance on the psychoanalytical viewpoints of Freudian thought. The F-scale describes a personality type marked by ethnocentric nationalism, extreme in-group conformity, rigid adherence to conventional values, submission to authority, a willingness to punish, opposition to the free-thinking and kind-hearted, arrogance toward those considered inferior, and other authoritarian attitudes that explain significant political outcomes (for instance, the rise of archconservative, ultranationalist, and fascist ideologies and war in twentieth-century Europe).

Political psychology benefited greatly from the "behavioral revolution" that swept the field of political science in the 1950s and 1960s and, in turn, was a key contribution to it. Researchers who were behavioralists focused their academic efforts on contemporary topics such examining how personality traits affect political engagement and party choice. Power, riches, well-being, skill, enlightenment, love, rectitude, and respect are just a few of the eight psychological justifications offered by Lasswell as to why people engage in politics. Similar to this, Robert E. Lane asserted in Political Life: Why and How People Get Involved in Politics that involvement in politics serves a variety of conscious and unconscious needs and motives, including power, monetary and material gain, friendship and affection, self-esteem, relief from psychic tensions, and a need to comprehend the wider world. From early studies like The People's Choice (1944), the well-known Austrian-born sociologist Paul F. Lazarsfeld's classic study of the 1940 U.S. presidential election, to later ones like The American Voter, the most well-known research study of American voting behavior by Angus Campbell, Philip

Converse, William Miller, and Donald Stokes, survey methods significantly improved as a result of the behavioral revolution. Election-related behavior was investigated in connection to different population and demographic factors (age, gender, level of education, type of employment, social class, ethnicity, race, religion, and ideology). Many in-depth analyses of belief systems, both at the mass and elite levels, have been conducted as a result of the increased sophistication of public opinion polling, such as Philip Converse's influential study, "The Nature of Belief Systems in Mass Publics" (in David Apter's Ideology and Discontent, 1964), which discovered that mass public opinion is frequently erratic, unstable, and uninformed.

Early political psychology had primarily focused on the unidirectional impact of individual and social psychological processes upon the polity, largely as a result of Lasswell's influence; however, in later decades, attention started to be devoted also to the reverse effect of politics on personality systems. Political systems' influence on people's behavior and ideals was examined in studies of political culture and political socialization, such as Gabriel Almond and Sydney Verba's The Civic Culture: Political Attitudes and Democracy in Five Countries. By the 1980s, the majority of political psychologists had come to terms with the "bidirectional" nature of the relationship between psychology and politics:

Whether they are citizens, leaders, group members, bureaucrats, terrorists, or revolutionaries, [people's] perceptions, beliefs, motives, opinions, values, interests, styles, defenses, and experiences are seen as influencing what they do politically. In turn, the political culture, political system, mechanisms of political socialization, political movements and parties, and the international system are seen as having an impact on what people are like. (1986, Hermann .p)

When the International Society of Political Psychology was established in 1978 and started hosting annual scientific conferences and publishing the quarterly journal Political Psychology, political psychology finally began to take form as an academic field in its own right. The study of voting behavior, political socialization, political leadership, the dynamics of public opinion, political attitudes, political cooperation and conflict, international negotiation, decision-making, and, more recently, the processing of political information, all make extensive use of psychological concepts.

The sample survey and the in-depth interview are the two empirical research techniques that are used the most often to explore psychological factors. For instance, political psychologists routinely employ attitude surveys to investigate the relationships between personality traits, population characteristics, and inclinations toward political engagement and party choice. The controlled experiment, focus groups, content analysis, simulation, and projective approaches are some further, more creative, but less often used research methodologies. Many political psychology research continue to be published within the context of allied social-science fields, particularly political science, demonstrating the pervasive and expanding tendency of applying psychological insights to political inquiry. Political psychology has already established a permanent, if somewhat heterogeneous and pluralistic, presence within the field of political science, despite the fact that there is no underlying scientific paradigm or even a single basic theory that gives this eclectic interdisciplinary field unity and coherence.

CHAPTER 4: REASONS WHY MEN ACQUIRE POWER

A person must have control over something or someone in order to have power over them.

One would assume that having the ability to influence others and shape events to match one's own reality would be appealing. (This obviously depends on who is in charge and what their vision is, so it might be good or harmful.) Yet, a recent research contends that those who aspire to power mostly want to exert control over one thing: themselves.

put out two distinct definitions of power: influence and autonomy. They claim that exercising control over others, which may include taking responsibility for others, is how power as influence is represented. Power as autonomy, on the other hand, "enables one to ignore and reject the influence of others and, so, to determine one's own destiny." Which of those goods, autonomy or influence, would sate people's need for power?

In the study's first phase, 100 participants completed an online survey in which the question: "Imagine you were granted a promotion at work." Others were told they had greater authority to choose their own objectives but less influence after receiving a promotion, while other participants were told the opposite. Neither possibility included a pay raise, and in both cases, their employer would be happy regardless of their decision. Just 28% of those in the higher-influence group said they would accept the promotion when offered, compared to 60% of those in the higher-autonomy group. In a follow-up poll when all participants were provided with both promos, the results were comparable.

The following experiment includes a 40 Spanish university students who came for an industrial training course. office role-playing, with some acting as managers and others as assistants. The participants were informed that they would have to execute a list of tasks some enjoyable, some tedious and that the managers would decide who among themselves and their aides would be in charge of each assignment. In a poll conducted after the fact, assistants claimed to be less content, to have less autonomy and influence, and to seek authority more than managers. Nonetheless, those helpers who felt the biggest lack of autonomy were more inclined to want control. The absence of influence didn't have the same impact as feeling it.

The need for more power is sated by autonomy, but not (or to a significant extent) by influence.

Next, participants were instructed to go back to a period when they had power over someone else or when they had authority over someone else in a series of priming trials, two with Americans and one with Indians (or what happened yesterday, as a control). They responded to questions on their satisfaction with their degree of control and authority after the event.

According to the researchers, having a sense of autonomy "quenches the need for further power but influence did not (or considerably less)" in all three trials.

Finally, the researchers conducted a survey of 986 readers of a Dutch magazine "aimed at professionals." Readers were asked to rate their level of power at work (as determined by where they stood in the company hierarchy), as well as their desire for more power, before completing surveys on the autonomy and influence that their positions afforded. Although middle managers, lower managers, and non-managers all expressed a desire for power at levels somewhat comparable to those of the top managers, top managers believed they had a great deal of autonomy and did not show a significant desire for it.

In conclusion, the results of this study suggest that the desire for power may be slightly misguided: In most cases, those who claim to seek authority really want autonomy. And once they have that freedom, they often lose interest in having power.

The self-determination hypothesis, a psychological theory that contends that, along with relatedness and competence, autonomy is one of humans' core psychological needs, supports the idea that individuals would prioritize autonomy above influence. According to this view, influence is not required. According to an another research, although aiming for power affects people's wellbeing, after they get it, they are actually happier because they feel more authentic their lives seem to be more in keeping with who they really are on the inside. It could be the case because having power allows people the independence to act as they like, which increases their feeling of wellbeing.

According to the authors of the current study, influence may seem more significant to individuals simply because it is more obvious. It is simpler to see how individuals manipulate others than it is to observe how they experience autonomy. The study claims that "the sense of autonomy of these powerful individuals is not as visible: It is reflected in the absence of constraint, plans not being thwarted, and ambitions not being frustrated an absence which remains unobserved." The study makes reference to real leaders like Napoleon, Caesar, Obama, and Putin as well as fictional ones like Darth Vader and Sauron.

This "may easily lead to a mistaken view of what motivates the desire for power," they said in their conclusion.

CHAPTER 5: THE THINGS MEN DO TO ATTAIN POWER

Getting into Power

Everyone is aware that some individuals have access to greater power than others. To achieve this, they:

do what is proper.
selecting the appropriate personnel.
Coalescing.
Co-opting.
Others.
Making the right decisions
While the majority of workers carry out their jobs as directed, effective and reliable role performance does not always translate into more influence.

For boosting personal strength, certain activities are noticeably superior than others. When a person's actions are unusual, highly visible, and particularly pertinent to organizational issues, their influence grows.

Exceptional Activities

Even when the performance is outstanding, routine work performance does not significantly increase personal power.

Individuals need to engage in unique or out-of-the-ordinary actions that often include some element of danger if they are to considerably grow their power.

A new contract, a new initiative, or a new product design are a few examples of unusual activity.

Transparent Activities

If no one is aware of extraordinary acts, they won't have much of an impact. In order for the unusual acts to be seen by others inside the company, ideally without the person needing to "Blow his own horn,"

Those who are forced to publicize their unusual actions do not acquire the same level of authority as those whose actions are reported by senior management or powerful outsiders.

Relevant Behaviors
The actions must not only be remarkable and noticeable, but they must also be seen as being crucial to the organization's purpose or the solution to significant organizational challenges.

Activities crucial to the existence of the organization do not result in the same level of personal power as trivial ones.

Making the Right People Available
People may strengthen their influence by forming informal connections with the appropriate people in addition to acting in the proper ways. Almost everyone, including supervisors, subordinates, and peers, may help an individual build their power if interpersonal ties are correctly handled.

Superiors

The adage "It's not what you know but who you know that matters" implies that a person's authority may be considerably increased by higher supervisors.

Mentors or sponsors are described as superiors who take a particular interest in and are eager to assist talented subordinates. Any higher-level officer or one of the immediate superiors may be one of these people.

By praising subordinates, suggesting them for new jobs, and making referrals to other powerful individuals, they may be very beneficial in boosting personal authority.

Subordinates

While it may seem strange for subordinates to have the ability to boost their superior's authority, they may have a big impact by supporting their superior's opinions and suggestions or by making them appear good.

Because of their reputation as excellent trainers and their ongoing relationships with their former subordinates, professors who educate bright doctorate students and managers who train exceptional new leaders may have a bigger effect.

Peers

Positive or negative peer interactions may either increase or decrease a person's power. People can't achieve on their own. They rely on the collaboration and support of their colleagues.

An adversarial relationship with peers may undermine one's sense of authority and keep them from contributing to the success of the company.

Coalescing

Putting together coalitions is another tactic used to gain and strengthen power. In order to achieve shared aims and objectives, individuals or organizations commonly pool their resources.

An alliance of this kind is mostly formed for the purpose of gaining more power to influence others via better resource management. A labor union, for instance, is made up of several people who fight to advance the interests of all employees.

Co-opting
Coopting is another strategy for boosting electricity. By placing persons or organizations whose support is required in positions of little authority, co-opting is done.

This strategy is distinct from consolidating in that it aims to neutralize dangers and challenges to a person's power base.

There are other ways to gain or strengthen power besides doing the right things, knowing the right people, consolidating, and co-opting. They serve as exemplars of the practices often seen and used in institutional contexts.

CHAPTER 6: IMPACT OF POWER ON THE MIND

There are several reports of strong guys acting inappropriately in the news. It's a sad but inevitable scene, and people in positions of authority can't help but take advantage of the situation. Of course, the issue is: Why does this horrific conduct occur? Why does power taint things?

This is referred to by psychologists as the power paradox. Once in a position of authority, a leader's same characteristics that helped them gain control in the first place almost completely vanish. They go from being kind, truthful, and outgoing to being impetuous, careless, and nasty. One of the main issues with authority, according to psychologists, is that it makes us less understanding of the worries and emotions of others. For example, numerous studies have shown that those in positions of authority are more likely to judge others using stereotypes and generalizations. They also make much less eye contact, at least when someone in authority is speaking.

Take a look at a recent study conducted by Northwestern University psychologist Adam Galinsky. In the beginning, Galinsky and colleagues asked participants to either describe a situation in which they felt like they had a lot of power or one in which they felt completely powerless. The subjects were then instructed by the psychologists to draw the letter E on their foreheads. At least when another person was present, those who had been primed with feelings of power were much more likely to draw the letter backwards. According to Galinsky et al., the myopia of power, which makes it very difficult to see things from another person's point of view, causes this impact. We write the letter backwards because we don't give a damn what other people think. What the maid thinks is irrelevant to us.

The problem is that we still believe we care, at least irrationally. That's because we become hypocrites very easily when we have power. In a 2009 study, Galinsky asked participants to consider a time when they had either power or had experienced powerlessness. After that, the students were split into two groups. On a nine-point scale, the first group was instructed to rank the moral gravity of underreporting business travel expenses. The number of lottery tickets each student received in the second group was determined by the outcome of a dice game in which they were asked to participate. More tickets resulted from a higher roll.

The high-power group members thought that failing to report travel expenses was a much worse offense. The outcome of the dice game, however, was wholly unexpected. In this case, respondents in the high-power group generally reported a result that was statistically unlikely, with an average dice score that was 20% higher than what would have been predicted by chance. (In comparison, the powerless group reported just marginally higher dice rolls.) This clearly implies that they were fabricating their true scores in order to get a few additional tickets.

Although though individuals nearly always understand that cheating is bad, it is nonetheless simpler for them to justify their unethical behavior because of their feeling of power. For instance, the high-power group consistently responded that it was worse when others committed those crimes than when they themselves did so when the psychologists asked the subjects (in both low- and high-power conditions) how they would judge someone who drove too fast while running late for an appointment. To put it another way, people who felt important believed that they had a good reason to speed because they were important people with important tasks to complete, but that everyone else should obey the posted signs.

However, these clever lab experiments, which were primarily conducted on the undergraduates might not have persuaded you. Maybe you feel that the paradigms are artificial. A psychologist ,She was curious about how our ability to reason was affected by our status. She discovered that the written opinions of justices tended to become less complex and nuanced as they gained power on the court or joined a majority coalition after studying more than a thousand decisions rendered by the US Supreme Court between 1953 and 1993. They took into account fewer angles and potential outcomes. Of course, the bad news is that the views expressed by the majority position end up being enacted as national law.

The main takeaway is that Foucault had a point when he said that the dynamics of power can have a significant impact on how we think. As we move up the social scale, our internal conflicts become distorted and we lose touch with our inherent empathy. We just act without worrying about how our actions will be perceived. What we desire, we merit. Moreover, how dare they object. Do they not recognize us?

Power is the degree of discretion and ability to compel others to act in accordance with one's own desires. According to this definition, power has two components:
Power over others refers to how many followers are reliant on and impacted by the acts of the leaders; power to impose one's will refers to the degree of discretion that leaders have to enforce their will over others. High power consequently entails, among other things, having more alternatives and sway over more people.

Lawrence Kohlberg's theory of moral growth, which contends that a person's assessment of what is morally good or wrong is impacted by how they reason about moral problems, is the most important theory on moral reasoning. Kohlberg's claim that moral thinking develops from infancy forward one step at a time, in an upward, progressive fashion, without missing a level or regressing to a previously learned stage, has come under heavy fire. In fact, several studies have shown evidence of stage regression, including cases when managers reacted less morally conscientiously to moral quandaries involving business decisions as opposed to non-business decisions or those involving psychological pain as opposed to physical harm. Based on these results, academics have suggested that moral growth should instead be seen as an extension of structures, during which time people retain their previously learned moral reasoning frameworks. So, moral evolution may be relatively malleable and susceptible to influences from socio-contextual elements that are unrelated to the dilemma's central theme, such as power.

Also, having authority allows the owner to act selfishly. For instance, prior research has shown that having authority increases people's propensity to utilize knowledge for their own gain, to make choices that improve their own rewards at the cost of their followers, or to act unethically (such as lying) when doing so benefits them. According to other research, when a choice would favor the person in power, people tended to stop relying on a moral code based on rules and instead turn to one that was outcome-oriented.

experimental planning

445 undergraduates of the management department from a medium-sized European institution to take part in an experiment to better understand power, self-interest, and moral thinking. Of of these participants, 177 were randomly allocated to one of four leader conditions (power over: 1 vs. 3 followers; power to: 3 vs. 4 reward possibilities), while the other students were placed in the follower position.

We defined self-interested behavior as the choice made by leaders considering the benefits for both themselves and their followers. With the default choice ("Option 1"), the rewards for the leader and follower would be equal at a cost borne by the leader, but in "Option 2," the payouts for the leader and follower would be equal at no cost to the leader (prosocial option). "Option 3" and "Option 4" indicate increasing leader compensation, but also a depletion of the public surplus since they reduce follower payouts (s).

In addition, a variety of made-up problems were offered to participants in the experiment (e.g. one dilemma is whether or not a doctor should administer an overdose of painkillers to a patient in pain). We asked them to decide how to proceed in these situations. Then, as a general indicator of moral reasoning, we arrived at a score (known as a "P-score") that reflected the proportion of items that made up Kohlberg's principled reasoning stages. This P-score reveals the extent to which people give post-conventional and ethical factors significant weight when making choices. A higher

P-score indicates a more principled and less selfish structure of moral reasoning.

Findings and relevant applications

We discovered that participants who had more followers were less likely to use moral reasoning structures that prioritized concerns for justice and the good of the group. However, participants who were given more (vs. fewer) payout options to control their followers did not differ in their moral reasoning, but they did have a stronger propensity to act in their own self-interest. More evidence that having more followers indirectly increased self-interested behavior by employing less morally rigorous moral reasoning structures was also discovered.

Understanding how power affects moral judgment and self-interested behavior is crucial from a practical standpoint for a number of reasons. First, moral decisions are frequently made in power imbalances and asymmetry, which makes self-interest seem more important. Second, high-ranking organizational leaders are often tasked with establishing and disseminating not just strategic goals but also the company's value system since they are seen as the primary sources of knowledge in organizations. Since they have an impact on employees as well as other stakeholders like suppliers and customers and eventually the society the organization works in, choices made by individuals in high power positions may thus be more significant than those made by those in lower power positions. But, our findings show that the more power one has, the less likely they are to take into account moral values of fairness and concern for the well of the whole.

Conclusions

Moral difficulties are among the most common and challenging problems that organizational leaders must solve. Solving moral problems sometimes involves making trade-offs between opposing but important beliefs, which contributes to the complexity. Another aspect of the challenge is that those in positions of power may be influenced in their moral reasoning and, as a result, in how they act. We discovered hints that power alters people's moral judgment, which leads to self-interested behavior. The two components of a leader's power includes number of followers and number of reward options do, however, seem to have separate consequences on moral judgment and, correspondingly, self-interested behavior. In conclusion, power should be investigated as a multifaceted phenomena in order to reveal its genuine nature.

CHAPTER 7: EFFECTS AND SOLUTIONS FOR POWER ABUSE

A leader who abuses their position of authority by acting inappropriately or with ulterior motivations. Some leaders attain extraordinary positions by disobeying the rules and forsaking the laws in their acts and undoings, in spite of all the institutions of government created to control their activities.

Some egotistical leaders plunder the public coffers and amass wealth at the expense of the general populace. They set the rules and extend their terms of office without respect for the law.

Effects: Anarchy, revolt, coup, underdevelopment, crises, political unrest, assassination, etc. are some of the main impacts of abuse of power. Politicians' adversaries develop negative sentiments when authority is abused.

Underdevelopment, exploitation, corruption, indiscipline, and other social evils are brought on by this circumstance.

Abuse of authority may result in chaos, insurrection, war, or even the dissolution of the state. Power-abusing leaders may sometimes be murdered. Large-scale repercussions result from power abuse, which is why many leaders are counseled against doing so.

Power abuse is harmful to the progress and development of any country. People's basic human rights are gravely infringed, and citizenship privileges are denied. resulting in persecution and tyranny. It raises the level of corruption in the country, which hinders economic growth. Resources intended for programs that improve the lives of people and the environment wind up in private wallets. Road systems, social facilities, and health services are still in terrible shape. Abuse of authority will eventually result in poor governance, which will open the door for officials to show disregard for the needs of the general public.

Solutions for Power Abuse Several actions need to be implemented in order to address the abuse of power in the country;

1. Cases of alleged abuse of authority must be thoroughly investigated, and the guilty parties must receive the proper punishment. The consequences might include suspension, promotion, or outright termination from the job.

2. The mass media, which serves as the fourth estate of the realm, should reveal and report on all forms of abuse of power in order to persuade individuals to stop doing it.

3. Periodic, fair elections must be held in order to ensure that elected political office holders are accountable to the voters.

4 The idea of judicial independence should be protected so that oppressed people may file lawsuits when their rights are violated.

5. The country should prioritize citizenship education. People should be taught how to be decent citizens who can aid in the growth of the country starting in the early stages of their schooling. People should be massively and intensively educated on ethical concerns by the National Orientation Agency and other pertinent Non-Governmental Organizations.

www.ingramcontent.com/pod-product-compliance
Lightning Source LLC
Chambersburg PA
CBHW050828250726
48653CB00006B/2485